A WALK DOWN THE FAIRWAY OF VALUE ADDED TAX

Third edition

by

IAN FLEMING, FIIT

First published January 2006 by Spiramus Press Ltd

© Spiramus Press Ltd, 2013

ISBN 978 1907444 75 3

This third edition published February 2013

www.spiramus.com

British Library Cataloguing-in-Publication Data.

A catalogue record for this book is available from the British Library.

The right of Ian Fleming to be identified as the author of this work has been asserted by him in accordance with the Copyright, Designs and Patents Act, 1988.

All rights reserved. No part of this publication may be reproduced in any material form (including photocopying or storing it in any medium by electronic means and whether or not transiently or incidental to some other use of this publication) without the prior written permission of the copyright owner except in accordance with the provisions of the Copyright, Designs and Patents Act 1988 or under the terms of a licence issued by the Copyright Licensing Agency Ltd, 90 Tottenham Court Road, London W1P 4LP.

Printed and bound in Great Britain by Berforts Information Press

Cover photograph courtesy of Carlisle Golf Club

CONTENTS

CONTENTS iii

FOREWORD ix

PREFACE xi

CHAPTER 1: THE STANCE 1

The Status of Golf Clubs 1

CHAPTER 2: THE GRIP 3

The VAT Exemption for competition and entry fees 3

CHAPTER 3: THE RULES OF GOLF 5

The VAT Exemption for Sport and Physical Recreation 5

CHAPTER 4: A BIRDIE OR AN EAGLE 7

1990 Refunds of VAT 7

CHAPTER 5: BUNKER PLAY 9

Partial Exemption 9

CHAPTER 6: DRIVER OR A NINE IRON 13

VAT Liability – taxable or exempt? 13

CHAPTER 7: THE HANDICAP SYSTEM 17

The VAT Legislation and liability of fees 17

    Meaning of "individual" 18

    Social Facilities 18

    Artisan Golf Clubs 19

    Governing Bodies 19

    Commercial Influence 20

CONTENTS

Emoluments 21

CHAPTER 8: MIXED FOURSOMES 23

Attribution of input tax to taxable supplies – some specific examples of club expenditure 23

The Clubhouse 23

Bar and Catering 25

The Course 27

CHAPTER 9: LOCAL RULES 29

Less common VAT rules 29

Gaming Machines 29

Lotteries 29

Entry Fees 30

Value of supplies 30

Prizes 31

Letting of Sports Facilities 32

The Golf Professional 32

CHAPTER 10: AN 18 HOLE PLAY-OFF 35

Recent decisions of the Courts and Tribunal that materially affect accounting for VAT by members' clubs 35

Action points 38

CHAPTER 11: MATCH PLAY – FINAL ROUND 39

Submission of claims for overpaid VAT 39

CONTENTS

CHAPTER 12: A VISIT FROM THE ROYAL AND ANCIENT GOLF CLUB 45

How to deal with a VAT inspection 45

CONCLUSION 49

APPENDIX A: Legislation Extracts 51

EC Sixth Directive, Article 13 51

Exemptions within the territory of the country 51

VATA 1994 52

Income and Corporation Taxes Act 1988 s. 839. 59

APPENDIX B: HMRC notices 61

Customs & Excise Business Brief 3/96 61

VAT exemption of non-profit making sports centres .. 61

HM Revenue & Customs Budget Notice BN 78 dated 12th March 2008 63

VAT: transitional period for claims 63

Revenue & Customs Brief 30/11 66

VAT: HMRC's position following the First-Tier Tribunal decision in the case of The Bridport and West Dorset Golf Club Limited 66

APPENDIX C: Golf Club VAT cases 69

EU Legislation 69

Keswick Golf Club and others v. Commissioners of Customs & Excise (No 15493) 24 February 1998 69

CONTENTS

Kennemer Golf & Country Club v. Staatssecretaris van Financien (Case C-174/00) 21 March 2002 (European Court of Justice) 70

Canterbury Hockey Club and Canterbury Ladies Hockey Club v. The Commissioners for HM Revenue and Customs 71

Whether or not a non-profit making body 73

De Vere Golf and Leisure Ltd and De Vere Group plc (No 18078) 8 April 2003 73

Chobham Golf Club v. Commissioners of Customs & Excise (No 14867) 26 March 1997 74

Recovery of input tax 75

Burntisland Golf House Club v. Commissioners of Customs & Excise (No 6340) 12 August 1991 75

Milnathort Golf Club v. Commissioners of Customs & Excise (No 17889) 11 November 2002 76

Elsham Golf Club Ltd. v. Commissioners of Customs & Excise (No 18107) 28 April 2003 77

VAT liability of income 78

Copthorne Village Golf Club v. Commissioners of Customs & Excise (No 17426) 5 October 2001 78

Abbotsley Golf and Squash Club Ltd v. Commissioners of Customs & Excise (No 15042) 2 May 1997 79

Different classes of membership 79

West Essex Golf Club v. Commissioners of Customs & Excise (No 7321) 28 February 1992 79

CONTENTS

Miscellaneous *80*

    Tall Pines Golf and Leisure Co. Ltd v. Commissioners of Customs & Excise (No 16538) 3 March 2000 80

    Cumbernauld Development Corporation v. The Commissioners of Customs & Excise (No. 14630) 6 November 2000 81

    Northampton Theatre Trust [2006] BVC 2587 83

Default Surcharge Assessments *84*

Table of Cases 85
Index 87

FOREWORD

"To that man, age brought only golf instead of wisdom" G B Shaw

As I have passed retirement age, I cannot deny that I am playing more golf than in former years, but my earlier sports pleasures of cricket and rugby are no longer an option for someone on the wrong side of sixty. I can also well remember being sent to Lytham St Annes VAT office for my formal VAT training in the late summer of 1973 having just taken up the frustrating game. I had been employed by the National Investigation Division of Customs & Excise with responsibility for the single VAT team in Birmingham, whilst everyone else was chasing drug smugglers, or so it seemed.

Bearing in mind that all VAT evasion was a criminal offence at this stage of the development of the tax, cases of evasion involving relatively little revenue (at the standard rate of 10%) took up time and effort unrelated to the tax at stake. My first "prosecution" related to £950 VAT when an Italian restaurant owner spent his suppressed takings renovating a DB4 Aston Martin.

I moved to the Lake District and joined Keswick Golf Club in 1979 and was immediately co-opted on to the Committee and Finance Sub-committee on the grounds that no one else in the Club knew anything about VAT! No one could have reasonably foreseen, at that time, the huge changes that were to overtake golf clubs in the next few years. By 1990, when the VAT liability of member's subscriptions changed,

FOREWORD

correctly, to being VAT exempt, I had been captain of the Club, and a member of the Committee for eleven years, and had just left Customs & Excise to join Armstrong Watson, the largest firm of Chartered Accountants in the North of England and Southern Scotland, outside the top four, as their Group VAT Specialist.

The firm had, and still has, a large number of golf club clients, with many partners and staff playing the game. Writing a book on the application of value added tax to members' golf clubs should, in theory at least, be easy. However, life is never easy, and as Gene Sarazen once said,

"Even when times were good, I realised that my earning power as a golf professional was dependent on too many ifs and putts"

Ian Fleming FIIT

PREFACE

The second edition was essentially an updating of the first edition following a number of Tribunal and Court decisions which were relevant to members' golf clubs. In particular, the implementation of the three year rule for submitting claims for overpaid output tax and underclaimed input tax, and it also reported the decision of the European Court of Justice (ECJ) in respect of the *Canterbury Hockey Clubs* (CHC)

The third edition reports on the stance taken by HM Revenue & Customs in respect of the very substantial number of appeals that have been submitted to the First Tier Tribunal, Tax, following the CHC decision and the subsequent rejection by HMRC of claims for large refunds of value added tax. It also considers the decision of the Upper Tribunal, Tax and Chancery Division, following an appeal by HMRC against the decision of the First Tier Tribunal in respect of *Bridport & West Dorset GC*, to refer the matter to the ECJ for guidance on the construction of articles 133(b) and 133(d) of Council Directive 2006/112.

HMRC are informing enquirers that a decision of the ECJ in this matter is unlikely to be received before mid 2013 at the earliest.

CHAPTER 1: THE STANCE

The status of golf clubs

I must start by setting out what I am trying to achieve by writing this book. There are basically three types of golf club. First, the private club, usually a corporate body, where the income earned from membership fees, and green fees obtained from casual visitors, generates profits which are distributed to the shareholders and/or owners. All such income in these circumstances is liable to value added tax (VAT) at the standard rate and generally does not create too much difficulty, although it can make membership more expensive than at an equivalent members' club.

The second type of golf club is one run by a local authority. When VAT was introduced in 1973, the then Chancellor of the Exchequer, The Rt. Hon. Anthony Barber MP, who was renowned for his famous statement that "VAT is a simple tax", made one other faux pas "VAT will not be a burden on the rates". As a result, the Finance Act 1972 had to be partially re-written to take into account the non-business activities of local authorities and in so doing, legislated for them to recover VAT charged to them that would not have been recoverable by a normal business.

The third type of golf club, and the most common, is the one with which this book is mainly concerned – the members' club – a not-for-profit organisation where any surpluses created on day-to-day activities cannot be distributed to members, or any other person except on the winding-up of the club, but can be used to maintain and/or improve the standard of facilities provided. When value added tax was introduced in 1973 as a condition of joining what was then called the Common Market, now the European Union, the UK was granted a derogation by that body from the EC Sixth Directive allowing the charging of VAT on subscriptions to members by organisations such as golf clubs. That derogation ran out on 31st December 1989 with the result that members' subscriptions became exempt from VAT from 1st January 1990, and all the problems that result from a business having both taxable and exempt income has resulted in this "simple tax" no longer being so for many treasurers of members' golf clubs. Hopefully, this book will help to allay the fears and difficulties that can arise and make the dreaded VAT inspection visit a less worrying occasion.

Although many doubts were expressed by VAT consultants as to whether the UK Government had correctly implemented the exemptions of the EC Sixth Directive, Article 13A(1)(m), little did they think that a ruling by HM Revenue & Customs (HMRC) refusing a refund of £433 would result in an appeal going all the way to the European Court of Justice (ECJ) and a decision that would create years of confusion and contradictions for members' clubs.

Finally, readers will be aware that the EC Sixth Directive, Articles 13A(1)(m) and 13A(2) have been replaced by Council Directive 2006/112 Articles 132 and 133 with no material amendment. The EC Sixth Directive is quoted where that was the extant legislation when the various appeals were considered.

CHAPTER 2: THE GRIP

The VAT Exemption for competition and entry fees

It is assumed that most readers of this book will have some knowledge of the basics of VAT legislation. In particular, it is a tax by exception where, provided supplies are made in the course or furtherance of a business, if they are not specifically liable at the lower or zero rates, or are exempt, they are liable to VAT at the standard rate – currently 20%.

It was not until 1980 that Customs & Excise (as they then were, now HM Revenue & Customs) introduced an exemption for competition and entry fees provided that all the income was returned to the competitors in the form of prizes including, where appropriate, cups and shields etc. as well as other goods, and the body was a non-profit making business or had charitable status.

Although the exemption was welcomed, there was a sting in the tale whereby the VAT cost of prizes and trophies was attributable to exempt income and, therefore, in principle, was not recoverable. Having said that, although the partial exemption *de minimis* limits (see Chapter 5) were not as helpful as they are today, most clubs were able to reclaim all the input tax attributable to these exempt supplies.

THE GRIP

A WALK DOWN THE FAIRWAY OF VAT

CHAPTER 3: THE RULES OF GOLF

The VAT Exemption for sport and physical recreation

It was apparent to many VAT specialists in early 1990 that, as a result of the derogation that had been granted to the UK in 1973 being withdrawn on 31st December 1989, the UK was now required to exempt

"certain services closely linked to sport or physical education supplied by non-profit making organisations, to persons taking part in sport or physical education"

(Article 13A(1)(m) of the EC 6th Directive)

Following concerted pressure by the accountancy profession in general, and VAT specialists in particular, Customs & Excise (now HMRC) issued a consultation paper on 30th September 1993 inviting views on the extension of the exemption in this area.

Customs & Excise eventually implemented Article 13 A(1)(m) into the Value Added Tax Act 1983 but limited the exemption to services supplied to members (excluding temporary members where membership was granted for periods of less than three months) on the grounds that under Article 13A(2), second indent, exemption must be withheld where the basic purpose is to raise additional income by carrying out transactions in direct competition with commercial organisations (see Appendix A). In the view of Customs & Excise, any income other than basic membership subscriptions was "additional".

In Business Brief 3/96 (dated 16 February 1996), Customs & Excise clarified their interpretation of a "membership scheme" (see Appendix B), with further clarification in VAT Notice 701/45 Sport – originally published in April 1994 and updated in April 2002.

The Customs & Excise view of membership was tested in a VAT Tribunal appeal by *Keswick Golf Club and Others* (No 15493) (see Appendix C) where it was argued that Keswick Golf Club, a members' club, was not in "direct competition" with commercial organisations and, as a result, all income including temporary memberships (often referred to as green fees) for the playing of golf [sport] should be exempt. The Tribunal failed to take the European legislation on board and made its decision entirely based on UK law which it believed was in accord with the EC Sixth Directive and the appeal was dismissed. There were substantial grounds for an appeal to a higher court but the appellants could not raise the necessary funds to take the case further where it might well have succeeded. For many years no other club took up the challenge on this point which was certainly not dead in the water.

No other club, that is, until *Canterbury Hockey Club* and *Canterbury Ladies Hockey Club* went all the way to the ECJ on an appeal against a refusal to repay £433. In allowing the Club's appeal, the ECJ went further than was requested in the referral and effectively ruled that to determine whether supplies of sporting services are VAT exempt, the identity of the recipients of the services is irrelevant. Detailed consideration of this decision is at Chapters 10 and 11.

CHAPTER 4: A BIRDIE OR AN EAGLE

1990 Refunds of VAT

One of the effects of the introduction of the exemption for subscriptions to non-profit making members' clubs was that they were invited to submit applications for a refund of VAT overpaid from 1st January 1990 as a result of the late implementation of the change. Following on from this, some very large claims were made and paid. It is perhaps relevant to point out here that at the time the legislation restricting the adjustment of errors to a maximum of three years had not been implemented, and the cost to the Exchequer of these repayments was a contributing factor, along with other large repayments in the pipeline, for the introduction of the three-year rule.

Another effect of the exemption was that whilst it would relieve members' golf clubs from the need to account for VAT on members' subscriptions, it would also result in a loss of input tax, particularly in respect of course maintenance and clubhouse refurbishment, as a result of the club becoming partially exempt.

There was an interesting concession by Customs & Excise that where a club owed an additional amount of VAT as a result of the change, Customs & Excise would waive the debt. This was most likely to occur when substantial expenditure on course or clubhouse developments was incurred, and the refund of VAT on membership fees was less than the input tax disallowed on the expenditure. Their generosity was almost unbelievable and has never been repeated as far as I am aware.

CHAPTER 5: BUNKER PLAY

Partial Exemption

As any good golfer will tell you, hitting a ball into a greenside bunker, whilst not recommended, is not a big problem so long as you know how to get out. The bunkers, in VAT terms, are the partial exemption rules which, like the golfing analogy, are easy to overcome if you know what they are and how to make sure that you are not buried by them.

This book, as is stated earlier, is concerned with the application of VAT to members' golf clubs – it is not a text book on VAT legislation. It is necessary, however, to remind readers of the current VAT partial exemption rules.

Essentially, the Value Added Tax Act 1994, section 24(5) states that input tax i.e. VAT incurred on purchases and expenses in the course or furtherance of a business, can only be reclaimed in so far as it is attributable to the making of taxable supplies i.e. activities liable to VAT at the standard, lower or zero rates. However, since the inception of VAT, HMRC have recognised that many businesses have small amounts of input tax attributable to exempt supplies and, if they had to calculate the amount of VAT that was not recoverable, the amount disallowed would be minimal in relation to both the complexity and time taken to undertake the calculations. Although never publicly stated by the Department, the time that would be taken up by VAT Officers checking the calculations would not be revenue efficient. As a result, partial exemption *de minimis* limits were set which, if not exceeded, meant the business could be treated as being fully taxable and all its input tax could be reclaimed. The history of partial exemption, as it is called, is not important to this book – suffice to say that the current limits are that the **exempt input tax** must not exceed £1,875 per quarter (£7,500 per annum) AND must be less than 50% of the total input tax incurred. If the exempt input tax falls below these limits, all the input tax can be reclaimed – if it doesn't fall below the limits, none of the exempt input tax is recoverable.

Just to make things a little more complicated, the calculations must be undertaken on a quarter by quarter basis, with an annual adjustment made at the quarter end nearest to the fiscal tax year, the adjustment being accounted for on the following quarter's return. HMRC will grant permission, on written request, for the annual adjustment to be undertaken to coincide with the club's financial year end.

The VAT liability of income received by a members' golf club is detailed in Chapter 6. Suffice to say here that, as far as golf is concerned, and in general terms, income from members is exempt, income from visitors is standard-rated, as is income from bar and catering irrespective of who is purchasing the product. Within these categories, however, there are a number of situations where great care needs to be taken when classifying the VAT liability as the obvious answer is not always correct, particularly now that we have the decision in *Canterbury Hockey Clubs* to consider.

From experience, it is only the very small members' clubs who are able to reclaim all their input tax under the partial exemption rules. The remainder have to put in place an accounting system that will correctly attribute expenditure to either taxable or exempt income. Every club has, of course, expenditure which cannot be directly attributed to either taxable or exempt income, for example accountancy fees and course maintenance – these have to be apportioned using the partial exemption "standard method", or, with the approval of HMRC, a "special method" that produces an equitable result. The standard method is essentially a *pro rata* calculation based on the ratio of taxable to total income. Special methods can be extremely complicated but for golf clubs, attribution of input tax on a sector basis e.g. course, clubhouse and administration can be used where the calculation results in a fair attribution acceptable to both HMRC and the club. HMRC's permission is not required to use the standard method but must be obtained to use a special method. In practice, special methods are not common in golf clubs as the standard method normally produces a fair result and is relatively simple to operate. If it doesn't, a special method should be applied for, after taking appropriate professional advice, but the issue is too complex, and dependent on the club's specific difficulties, to be considered here.

BUNKER PLAY

CHAPTER 6: DRIVER OR A NINE IRON

VAT Liability – taxable or exempt?

Clearly, if the correct choice of club is not made, the ball will not land where it is intended, and choosing the incorrect liability for your income can result in very substantial assessments, penalties and interest for VAT purposes if picked up by an HMRC Officer looking at the last three years' VAT returns. A word of warning, which should not be necessary, but if the understatement amounts to deliberate evasion, the tax can be assessed for past periods up to twenty years!

Liability is best looked at from a course/clubhouse point of view – being further analysed into member/non-member categories. See Chapter 7 below for an explanation of the term "eligible body".

The table overleaf sets out the VAT liability of the activities normally associated with a golf club.

Nature of the Service

Nature of the Service	Supply by "eligible" body To members	Supply by "eligible" body to non-members pre CHC[1]	Supply by "eligible" body to non-members post CHC
Use of changing rooms, showers, locker hire etc	*Exempt*	*Standard-rated*	*Exempt*
Permission to use the golf course and other playing facilities	*Exempt*	*Standard-rated*	*Exempt*
Use of other sports Facilities	*Exempt*	*Standard-rated*	*Exempt*
Coaching services	*Exempt (this excludes supplies by a self-employed golf professional but see paragraph (a) below*	*Exempt*	*Exempt*
Membership Subscriptions and joining fees covering active participation in sport	*Exempt*	*n/a*	*n/a*

[1] CHC refers to Canterbury Hockey Clubs decision.

Social or non-playing Subscriptions	Standard-rated	Standard-rated	Standard-rated
Fees for remaining on a waiting list for membership	Standard-rated or exempt. See paragraph (b) below.	Standard-rated or exempt. See paragraph (b) below	Standard-rated or exempt. See paragraph (b) below
Admission charges for Spectators	Standard-rated	Standard-rated	Standard-rated
Use of residential Accommodation	Standard-rated	Standard-rated	Standard-rated
Use of transport	Standard-rated	Standard-rated	Standard-rated
Catering, bars, gaming machines and social functions	Standard-rated	Standard-rated	Standard-rated
Match fees for the use of playing facilities	Exempt	Standard-rated	Exempt
Match fees covering the cost of catering and transport	Standard-rated	Standard-rated	Standard-rated
Parking	Standard-rated	Standard-rated	Standard-rated

(a)   Sports Coaching

Sports coaching by professionals is not within the exemption as it is not supplied by an "eligible body".

However, such coaching may qualify for the exemption for education. See VAT Notice 701/30 Education and vocational training. (See also Chapter 9, Golf Professional)

(b) Joining Fees

A charge to be placed on a waiting list is exempt if:

- it is deducted from the new member's first subscription or entrance fee and the entrance fee or subscription will itself qualify for exemption; and
- it is refundable in the event that the candidate fails to become a member for any reason, including voluntary withdrawal.

In all other circumstances the fee is consideration for the right to be on the waiting list and is standard-rated.

CHAPTER 7: THE HANDICAP SYSTEM

The VAT Legislation and liability of fees

As explained in Chapter 1, this book is aimed at helping members' golf clubs' officials to keep their VAT liabilities to a minimum and avoid disputes with HMRC. It has to be stated here, however, that some privately owned clubs have attempted over the years to set up members' clubs under their "control" and, as a result, HMRC have had to draft anti-avoidance legislation to ensure that only genuine members' clubs are able to take advantage of the exemptions from VAT.

The law is contained principally in the Value Added Tax Act 1994, Schedule 9, Group 10, and the Income and Corporation Taxes Act 1988 s.839 which is cross-referenced to Group 10 (see Appendix A).

The VAT exemption relates to certain sporting and physical education services provided by eligible bodies, and entry to certain competitions in sport or physical recreation. An eligible body is defined as one that
- **is non-profit making; and**
- **its constitution includes a non-distribution clause or limits its distribution to:**
  - another non-profit making club;
  - its members on winding up or dissolution; and
- **actually uses all profits or surpluses from its playing activities to maintain or improve the related facilities or for the purposes of a non-profit making body; and**
- **is not subject to commercial influence.**

THE HANDICAP SYSTEM

The above-quoted legislation does raise a number of VAT liability issues which are now considered.

Meaning of "individual"

For the purposes of the exemption, an individual is a person who actually takes part in the sporting or physical education activity and this includes:
- family groups, and
- informal groups where one individual makes a booking on behalf of a group of users of the sporting facilities.

The following are NOT supplies to individuals:
- by a club to one of its sections where the individual section has a separate and independent constitution e.g. the golf section of a multiple-sports club; or
- to travel agents or tour operators that have agreements with the club to supply the use of sporting facilities to individuals, groups, or corporate bodies.

BUT see Chapter 10 following the decision in *Canterbury Hockey Clubs* for alternative considerations.

Social Facilities

Social facilities supplied to members on payment of a subscription are standard-rated. Where a subscription covers both sporting and social facilities, it should, in principle, be apportioned between the exempt and standard-rated supplies. However, there is an exception for non-profit making (eligible) bodies which supply a mixture of benefits with different VAT liabilities. As a concession they **may** apportion their subscriptions to reflect the value and VAT liability of each individual benefit, even if they are consideration for a single supply. This concession is explained in more detail in VAT Notice 701/5 Clubs and Associations.

Artisan Golf Clubs

Membership fees charged to members of artisans' golf clubs are exempt from VAT. An artisans' club is a members' club that shares the playing facilities with another members' club, normally for a consideration, and golf is usually restricted to the Monday to Friday period. Charges made by the host club to an artisans' golf club and its members were standard-rated but are now considered to be exempt following *Canterbury Hockey Clubs*. If artisan golfers are members of the main club, or it is the artisans' golf club which supplies the right of play to its members, charges for the use of the golf course are exempt.

Governing Bodies

Affiliation fees payable to, for example, The English Golf Union and other equivalent bodies in Scotland, Wales and Northern Ireland, are re-charged to members. This is because the affiliation fee is calculated on a basis which relates to an individual (e.g. per person based on the number of members), and the services provided are closely linked to the sport. Affiliation fees are thus exempt.

In order to avoid discrimination between private and members' clubs, by concession HMRC allow affiliation fees to be treated as disbursements if shown separately on invoices issued for annual subscriptions.

Taking into account the above, it does make one wonder why HMRC refused the repayment claim by *Canterbury*

Hockey Clubs that resulted in the appeal going all the way to the ECJ.

Commercial Influence

This is a much more complicated matter and VAT Notice 701/45 Sport (April 2002) considers this in detail.

Essentially, a club is considered to be under commercial influence if, in the three years leading up to the time of a supply, a "relevant supply" was made to the club, an "emolument" was paid by the club, and/or an agreement exists for:

"the grant of either any interest in or right over land or licence to occupy any land which at any time in the relevant period was, or was expected to become, sports land; and in the case of Scotland, of any personal right to call for or to be granted any such interest or right; *or* **of the use of sports land (that is, where rent is paid) under leases granted, varied or renewed after 31 March 1996,** *or* **the supply of any services in managing or administering any of its facilities,** *or* **the supply of any goods or services for more than the normal market price."**

Supplies made by a charity or local authority, or made by a company to a club owned by that company and whose principal purpose is to provide employees of that company with sports facilities, are not "relevant supplies". Similarly, a gift of sports land, a supply of sports land made in return for a nominal amount, and a supply of the use of sports land, provided that the original grant of land was also made for a nominal amount, are not "relevant supplies". As a general guide, HMRC will accept any amount not exceeding £1,000 to be a nominal amount.

Emoluments

Emoluments include all salaries, fees, wages, and profits, however calculated, but do not include genuine honoraria paid in return for services rendered to the club by Officers appointed at General Meetings.

THE HANDICAP SYSTEM

CHAPTER 8: MIXED FOURSOMES

Attribution of input tax to taxable supplies – some specific examples of club expenditure

Having explained in Chapter 5 the concept of direct attribution, it is essential to ensure that input tax attributable to taxable supplies is calculated in the most tax-efficient manner within the rules of the game. In addition, however, there are some often forgotten sources of income and expenditure that can have disastrous effects on input tax recovery.

The Clubhouse

Despite the success of *Milnathort Golf Club* at the VAT and Duties Tribunal (see Appendix C), it is very important that your architects and builders "think VAT" when designing and undertaking major refurbishments to clubhouses.

It is normally possible to split a clubhouse into at least three distinct areas – bar/lounge, dining area and locker rooms. In general terms any VAT attributable to the dining room will be fully recoverable as it should only be used for making taxable supplies. Equally, input VAT incurred in the bar area is recoverable, as the sale of drinks and incidentals like crisps and nuts are liable to VAT at the standard rate. The locker rooms, on the other hand are used for both taxable (visitors') and exempt (members') supplies and the input VAT should be treated as being residual and included in the pot for partial exemption purposes, although following the

Canterbury Hockey Clubs decision, all locker room expenditure will be attributable to exempt supplies.

It is important, therefore, that any contractors working on more than one part of the building should itemise their charge to each area, when preparing their VAT invoice to the club, to ensure a direct attribution to taxable and exempt supplies. Some clubs separate members' and visitors' locker rooms, often for reasons unconnected with VAT, and it still makes good sense from a VAT point of view if major works are planned that way even if the *Canterbury Hockey Clubs* decision disallows the recovery of input VAT on temporary members' accommodation.

Two warnings, however, should be made. The first follows the case of a Scottish golf club which undertook a massive clubhouse renovation and the snooker table was situated in the bar area. A visiting VAT inspector said that because the bar area was used for making both taxable and exempt supplies, a significant amount of VAT had to be transferred into the pot instead of being fully recoverable, and a large assessment was the result. The exempt income was only about 1% of total income but the decision resulted in a 50% loss of VAT on the bar area refurbishment. Snooker tables and dart boards should be in separate games rooms wherever possible to avoid this problem.

The second warning relates to the Tribunal decision in *Elsham Golf Club Ltd* (see Appendix C) who renovated their dining room and then admitted to the VAT inspector, and the VAT and Duties Tribunal, that the dining room was used for meetings of the club members, and was used by members for socialising and relaxing whether or not food and drink was purchased. It was ruled that the dining room was not used exclusively for making taxable supplies, the input tax was not attributable to taxable supplies, and should be treated as residual. Again, this cost the club a considerable amount of money.

Bar and Catering

In most members' clubs, catering is provided to members, guests and visitors and this is usually provided by a steward and/or catering manager. It is not uncommon for a husband and wife team to be appointed where one looks after the bar and the other provides the catering service. This arrangement, if not thought through from a VAT point of view, is fraught with danger.

No two clubs are the same, but the scenario often goes along the following lines. A husband and wife team is appointed on an annual retainer. In return, the husband is the bar steward and employs such staff as is necessary to assist him, paying their wages from the retainer. His wife has the free use of the club kitchen but is responsible for the purchase of food and the employment of staff as necessary. Bar takings are retained by the club, catering income is retained by the steward's wife.

The picture can be made even more complicated if the steward and wife occupy a flat in the clubhouse, or some other dwelling on the course, rent-free. In return they are normally expected to be responsible for the security of the premises. The VAT issues of this arrangement can be extremely complex and the VAT status of the husband and wife team cannot be overlooked. Are they in partnership, or are they providing their services as two sole traders? If so, are they both registered for VAT purposes? It is an easy answer to say that it is their problem – it may be from a legal viewpoint but it doesn't stop the matter impinging on the club's VAT position. The wife, as the provider of catering is virtually bound to be VAT registered, but her husband may be able to operate just below the VAT registration limit (currently a turnover of £77,000).

In the above circumstances, can the club reclaim VAT on the refurbishment of the kitchen and/or the steward's accommodation? Not necessarily, according to HMRC and, to be fair, it is difficult to argue that the input tax incurred on the kitchen is incurred in the course or furtherance of the club's business as opposed to the business of the caterer; and the accommodation is provided to the steward and his wife for their private purposes. There may be some benefit to the club but that is not sufficient for VAT recovery – the input tax has to be incurred in the course or furtherance of the business as stated above.

With careful attention to the details of the contract, the problem can be largely overcome. If a "catering concession" is granted to the caterer for an annual sum plus VAT, the retainer to the steward can be increased by a similar amount with the result that the net payment to the steward and his wife remains the same. The refurbishment of the kitchen is now attributable to a taxable supply and all the input VAT is recoverable.

Rent-free accommodation can cause tax problems for the steward as well as VAT issues for the club, and it is a matter for the professional advisors to both parties to decide how best to deal with this issue.

ATTRIBUTION OF INPUT TAX TO TAXABLE SUPPLIES

The Course

As the course is clearly used by members and temporary members alike, it is clear that any associated input tax is residual and must be apportioned using the standard method explained in Chapter 5, or such other method as may be agreed with HMRC, but following the *Canterbury Hockey Clubs* decision, all input tax on course development and upkeep will be attributable to exempt supplies and therefore non-deductible.

It may be, however, that special events are held during the year e.g. Pro Am tournaments or even a full professional event such as an Open Qualifying tournament. The income received by the club, either from the competitors or, in the latter case, from the R&A at St. Andrews is liable to VAT at the standard rate. The VAT on any extra expenditure incurred specifically for these events is attributable to a taxable supply and is recoverable in full. This is easily justified as the Committee will want the course to be in first class condition for the event and may hire extra grass cutting equipment, purchase ropes and stakes for spectator control, or even hire temporary grandstands for public use. The club must ensure that its accounting system can clearly identify such extra expenditure, and recover the VAT accordingly.

MIXED FOURSOMES

CHAPTER 9: LOCAL RULES

Less common VAT rules

These are rules which are in force but are usually hidden away on a notice board in the clubhouse and which members often forget are there unless it is to their advantage. In VAT terms, there are VAT rules which are published in legislation and public notices, but club treasurers and committees don't know they are there until they fall over them.

Gaming Machines

HMRC Officers are very good at taking the back off gaming machines and reading totalisator figures to compare machine takings with the declarations in your cash book. You have been warned.

Lotteries

Many clubs use lotteries as fund-raising events on a regular basis – often in association with other activities in the clubhouse. No problem with that – income from lotteries is exempt from VAT. However, if a major refurbishment of the clubhouse has just taken place, and the bar area is used for lottery purposes, the input tax on the refurbishment is no longer solely attributable to the making of taxable supplies (bar sales) and the VAT Officer can argue that the input tax on the bar refurbishment should be treated as residual and added to the "pot" rather than be recovered in full.

LOCAL RULES

Entry Fees

An entry fee for the right to enter a competition is basically liable to VAT at the standard rate. However, the right to enter a competition in "sport or physical recreation" is exempt where the grant is made by an eligible body. There is little doubt that a members' golf club falls within the above exemption.

Value of supplies

If entry to a competition includes a meal in the clubhouse after participating, it is necessary to decide whether a single or multiple supply is being made. Following the decision in *Card Protection Plan v. Commissioners of Customs & Excise*, if the value of the meal is incidental to the supply of the right to take part in the competition, then the whole cost can be treated as exempt when provided to a member of the club.

If the competition is an open competition i.e. members from any club can compete, everyone's entry fee is liable at the standard rate. Provided the event is clearly not a fund-raising event, it may be possible to argue following the ECJ decision in *Canterbury Hockey Clubs*, that all the income is exempt but much would depend on the reasons for promoting the event.

Where charity events are being organised, it makes sense for the club to make the facilities available free of charge to the charity, and allow a fundraiser who is not registered for VAT, to organise the event, subject of course to committee control. Under different legislation, charities are allowed themselves to organise fund-raising events exempt from VAT and this is another option that can be used –

particularly if the entry fee is high, and an after-golf dinner is being provided with professional entertainment.

Prizes

Where the entry fee for a competition is in money which is allocated *wholly* towards the provision of a prize or prizes awarded in that competition, the income is exempt from VAT (VATA 1994, Schedule 9, Group 10, Item 1). If all or any of the entry fees are carried forward as prizes in other competitions, the entry fee for the original competition is outside the scope of the exemption and is *standard-rated*.

It is recognised that many VAT Officers turn a blind eye to the carrying-forward of prize money so long as all the money is returned to competitors in prizes or trophies in the same season or financial year, particularly as prizes often have to be purchased in advance of the competition and it is administratively difficult to match entry fees to prizes exactly. Great care needs to be taken that any difference between the two amounts on a competition by competition basis is kept as small as possible.

The accounting for VAT on the purchase of prizes awarded to competitors is the same irrespective of whether the entry fees are exempt or standard-rated.

a. Goods

These are treated as business gifts. No output VAT is due on prizes costing £50 or less, and the input tax on their purchase can be reclaimed. Where the goods cost more than this, output VAT must be paid on the cost of the prize but the input tax incurred on the purchase can be deducted.

LOCAL RULES

b. Cash Prizes (or vouchers)
These are outside the scope of VAT.

c. Trophies
Loans of any type of trophy which remain the property of the club hosting the competition, is a supply of services but, because there is no consideration, the supply is outside the scope of VAT.

Letting of Sports Facilities

The letting of facilities designed or adapted for the playing of sport is normally standard-rated. Thus the letting of a golf course to a company for a fee so that it can entertain its staff and business guests is liable to VAT at the standard rate even if some of the people playing are members of that club.

The Golf Professional

In most members' clubs, a golf professional is appointed both to sell golfing goods to the members and visitors, but also to provide teaching services to anyone requiring them. It is normal for the club to provide accommodation for the professional in the form of a shop and/or workshop facilities for repairing golf clubs etc.

Financial arrangements can vary, but usually there are two distinct supplies. The Club pays the professional an annual retainer (usually made in stage payments) to assist him in providing his services to members at a competitive price, but also to collect green fees from visitors (temporary members), as well as administering the running of club competitions. As golf professionals are invariably registered

LESS COMMON VAT RULES

for VAT, a VAT invoice should be made out to the club by the professional for these supplies.

Whether or not the VAT can be reclaimed as input tax will depend on the contract. If the payment is made purely for the collection of green fees, it is attributable to a taxable supply and is recoverable in full. If it is partly for this service and also for the provision of other services to members, HMRC could argue that the input tax is residual and should be included in the "pot" for partial exemption purposes. The wording of the contract is all important here. If the professional acts as unofficial starter out of the goodness of his heart, and not under any contractual liability, and the retainer is clearly paid in respect of the collection of green fees, HMRC cannot argue that the input tax is not deductible.

The provision of coaching by the golf professional is not exempt from VAT under Group 10 as the supply is not made by an eligible body to the member. However, the Value Added Tax Act 1994, Schedule 9, Group 6, Item 2 exempts the supply of private tuition in a subject ordinarily taught in a school or university, by an individual teacher acting independently of an employer. HMRC have accepted that golf is now a subject ordinarily taught in a university as a number offer scholarships in golf studies. Teaching by a professional is thus exempt under this provision.

Most assistant professionals are employed and paid by the professional for assisting with the running of the professional's shop. In order to take advantage of the exemption for teaching detailed above, they usually act as self-employed persons for teaching purposes.

LOCAL RULES

CHAPTER 10: AN 18 HOLE PLAY-OFF

Recent decisions of the Courts and Tribunal that materially affect accounting for VAT by members' clubs

In Chapter 3 reference is made to the VAT Tribunal appeal by *Keswick Golf Club and Others* (see also Appendix C) and, in particular, the inability of the Club to take the matter to a higher court due to financial considerations. Little did VAT consultants think at that time that an appeal by *Canterbury Hockey Club and Canterbury Ladies Hockey Club* against a refusal by HMRC to repay a claim for £433 in respect of VAT paid on affiliation fees to England Hockey would result in a decision of the ECJ that would substantially change the generally accepted view of the VAT liability of members' golf clubs income. This case is discussed in more detail in Chapter 11 and at Appendix C.

The other recent relevant case, *Michael Fleming (trading as Bodycraft) and Conde Nast Publications Ltd*, settled a long-running argument that followed the introduction on 17th July 1996 of what is commonly referred to as the three-year rule for the recovery of overpaid output tax, or underclaimed input tax.

Substantial legal argument followed. In particular, the ECJ ruled in 2002 in *Marks & Spencer v Customs & Excise Commissioners* (Case C-62/00) that the introduction of the three-year cap in s.80 of VATA 1994 without an adequate transitional period breached Community law rights and so was invalid.

HMRC's reaction was to implement a three-month transitional period for claims which required that the taxpayer must have been aware of the right to claim before 31st March 1997, and to have made a claim before 31st March 2003.

Further legal argument ensued, resulting in the decision of the House of Lords in January 2008 in *Fleming (trading as Bodycraft) v Revenue and Customs Commissioners; Condé Nast Publications Ltd v Revenue and Customs Commissioners* ([2008] UKHL 2) that, because there was no transitional period when the three-year cap was first introduced, the cap had no effect for claims for over-declared output tax in accounting periods ending between 1st April 1973 and 4th December 1996.

Following this decision, HM Revenue & Customs were obliged to introduce a belated transitional period for making claims under s.80 arising between 1st April 1973 and 4th December 1996. The transitional period was announced in the March 2008 Budget and expired on 31st March 2009. Details of the transitional arrangements are to be found in Budget Notice 78 which is reproduced in Appendix B.

The decision of the ECJ in *Canterbury Hockey Clubs* then followed which resulted in the submission of a large number of claims for overpaid VAT, and legal arguments in the Tax Tribunals are far from finished.

It is, perhaps, relevant to point out here that the use of the words "green fee" is not helpful. Visitors pay a green fee in order for them to become temporary members of the Club and this allows them to purchase alcohol from the bar without the Club contravening the licensing regulations.

So what does the *Canterbury Hockey Clubs* decision mean for members' clubs? As far as affiliation fees are concerned, the home golf unions did not charge VAT to member clubs and so the arguments put forward re England Hockey are not relevant to golf clubs. But, as stated earlier, the ECJ went much further than was expected in answering the referral made by the hockey clubs.

In brief they made two rulings in their decision

1. **Article 13A(1)(m) of the Sixth Council Directive... includes services supplied to corporate persons and to unincorporated associations, provided that – which it is for the national court to decide – those services are closely linked and essential to sport, that they are supplied by non-profit-making organisations and that their true beneficiaries are persons taking part in sport.**

2. **The expression "certain services closely linked to sport", in Article 13A(1)(m)... does not allow the member States to limit the exemption under that provision by reference to the recipients of the services in question.**

A further point, confirmed by the ECJ in the decision in *Kennemer Golf & Country Club v. Staatssecretaris van Financien (Case C-174/00) of 21st March 2002* (see Appendix C), is that an organisation might be categorised as non-profit making even if it systematically sought to achieve surpluses which it then used for the purposes of the provision of its services. It is not difficult to argue that temporary membership fees would fall into that category. If the income received is only used for improving the services provided by the golf club to its "members", the direct competition argument has little credence bearing in mind that commercial organisations are

AN 18 HOLE PLAY-OFF

fully taxable and can reclaim input tax incurred on all their activities.

Any claim paid will, of course, be subject to interest as well – a not inconsequential amount for claims going back to 1st January 1990.

Action points

1. If your club has not considered lodging a claim for a refund of VAT on temporary members fee income, you could be losing a lot of money. Can you afford not to make a claim?

2. Discuss your potential claim, taking into account the advice given in this book, with your accountants.

3. Remember that if you intended to make a claim for the period 1st January 1990 to the 4th December 1996, that claim had to be made by the 31st March 2009, but that does not preclude you from making a claim for the last three years which could still be substantial.

4. Consider pages 37-38 very carefully. There is a period of approximately eight years between the 4th December 1996 and, say, the 31st December 2004 – the beginning of, the now legal, three year period. Even if a claim for this period was rejected by the VAT & Duties Tribunal and/or the Courts, it would not invalidate your claim for the earlier and later periods.

5. When calculating your claim, don't forget to claim interest as well but leave it to HMRC to undertake the actual calculations.

CHAPTER 11: MATCH PLAY – FINAL ROUND

Submission of claims for overpaid VAT

The reason that members' golf clubs (and other similar sporting organisations) are now in a position to make a claim for overpaid VAT follows from the decision of the ECJ in *Canterbury Hockey Clubs*. Put simply, the Court ruled that in order to determine whether supplies of sporting services were VAT exempt, the identity of the recipient of those services was irrelevant. Therefore, the UK legislation applying to non-profit making members' clubs that differentiates between members (VAT exempt) and temporary members (standard rated) is incorrect.

The next question to be considered is whether members' golf clubs have a claim for a refund of output tax relating to the period 1st April 1973 to the 4th December 1996. Customs & Excise (now HMRC) acting under an EU Derogation, introduced legislation when the UK joined what was then known as The Common Market, that standard–rated income from members and temporary members alike. After this derogation expired, on the 31st December 1989 (see page 2), Customs & Excise argued that they were still entitled to continue standard rating the income, but they were finally persuaded to change their view in 1996, resulting in large refunds of VAT overpaid in respect of subscriptions received from members. There is a strong argument that this repayment should also have included VAT paid on green fees collected after 1st January 1990.

MATCH PLAY – FINAL ROUND

So what does the *Canterbury Hockey Clubs* decision mean for members' clubs? As far as affiliation fees are concerned, the home golf unions did not charge VAT to member clubs and so the arguments put forward re England Hockey are not relevant to golf clubs. But, as stated above, the ECJ went much further than was expected in answering the referral made by the hockey clubs – in particular, that the identity of the recipient of the sporting services was irrelevant in determining whether or not a supply was exempt.

There are, therefore, substantial grounds for submitting a claim on the basis that the distinction between members and non-members is illegal and, provided the members' club is a genuine non-profit making organisation, income from temporary members as well as full members is exempt from VAT.

There are, however, two riders to this decision which HMRC may seek to use to reject a claim. First, paragraph 33 of the ECJ decision states that

"Finally, it is important to point out that, under the second indent of Article 13A(2)(b) of the Sixth Directive, services are not to be granted exemption under Article 13A(1)(m) if their basic purpose is to obtain additional income for the organisation by carrying out transactions which are in direct competition with those of commercial enterprises liable for VAT."

Secondly, HM Revenue & Customs might use the "unjust enrichment" argument to reject any claim. (VATA 1994, s.80(3)).

The first argument will clearly depend on the facts and circumstances of each claim but is defensible by competent legal advisors. The author has already seen legal arguments in another case that a non-profit making organisation cannot be unjustly enriched as any refund of overpaid VAT belongs to their members and is not capable of being paid or repaid to anyone else. For that reason, also, it is important that visitors are classified as temporary members.

Following the publication of BN 78, a claim can be made for overpaid output tax from 1st January 1990 to 4th December 1996, and also for the three years immediately preceding the submission of the claim to HMRC. It should be noted, however, that any claim for the period 1st January 1990 to 4th December 1996 had to be submitted by 31st March 2009 at the latest – the end of the new transitional period.

This, however, is not the end of the matter. If it is accepted from the ECJ decision that the UK failed to implement correctly the exemption from VAT under the EC Sixth Directive, Article 13A(1)(m), then, following the decision in *Northampton Theatre Trust* [2006] BVC 2587, (see Appendix C) where the company was deemed to have had a Community law right to repayment of the VAT paid in error, any claim following *Canterbury Hockey Clubs* made by any members' golf club, should be in respect of VAT returns submitted for the whole period 1st January 1990 to the date of submission of the claim.

Because of the large number of appeals submitted, the First Tier Tribunal (Tax), following rejection of claims by HMRC, of its own volition (but presumably with the agreement of HMRC), decided to hear two "test cases". The first was *Bridport & West Dorset Golf Club* (TC 01214), before Judge Colin Bishopp which was reported on the 1st June 2011. It is relevant that he also chaired the *Keswick Golf Club* appeal to the VAT & Duties Tribunal in 1998 which he made reference to in his decision in *Bridport & West Dorset Golf Club*. His conclusion that

"The exclusions from exemption of art. 134 of the Principal VAT Directive do not apply to the appellant's supplies. I recognise that in so concluding, I am departing from my earlier decision in Keswick Golf Club. The attempt by the domestic legislation to implement art. 133d of the Directive is ineffective, and does not take the appellant's supplies of the right to play golf in exchange for green fees, out of the exemption."

This was a bitter blow to HMRC but they were subsequently granted leave to appeal to the Second Tier Tribunal.

After a substantial delay for reasons unknown, the second test case, *Chipping Sodbury Golf Club* (TC 02234) was heard, and reported on the 30th August 2012. The Club was joined in the appeal by *The Dyke Golf Club* – another members' club, and by *Trent Lock Golf Club* and *Mendip Spring Golf & Country Club* – both proprietary clubs operated for the benefit of the proprietors.

The issues in dispute were totally different from *Bridport & West Dorset Golf Club*, namely, whether a member's subscription was for a single or multiple supply, and whether, in respect of the proprietary clubs only, they were entitled to exemption for some of their income, and, in particular, whether a restriction confirming the exemption only to non-profit making clubs is unlawful because it distorts competition and breaks the principle of fiscal neutrality. *Chipping Sodbury Golf Club's* appeal was concentrated on pre 1st January 1990 income. *Trent Lock Golf Club* had submitted a claim for repayment from 1992 to 2008, and *Mendip Spring Golf & Country Club* from 1993 to 2008.

In his conclusion, the Tribunal Judge, David Demack, felt satisfied that at all material times there had been a single supply of services by each of the appellants, and that supplies by the proprietary clubs after 1st January 1990 had been properly liable at the standard rate.

The appeal to the Upper Tribunal, Tax & Chancery Chamber by HMRC was heard by The Hon. Mrs Justice Proudman DBE and was reported on the 30th July 2012 when she referred the appeal to the ECJ for clarification of the relevant paragraphs of the Sixth Directive. In a complex decision she decided, after considering the judgment of Lord Denning MR in *HP Bulmer Limited v J Bollinger SA* [1974] Ch 401, that there should only be a reference if it is necessary in order to enable the court to give judgment, she decided to refer both issues as to the construction of art.134(b) (whether the basic purpose of the supply is to obtain additional income) and art.133(d) (whether the exemptions must not be likely to cause distortion of competition).

Bearing in mind that Counsel for HMRC in the *Keswick Golf Club* case argued strongly (and successfully at that time) that they were entitled to standard-rate income from temporary memberships, it is considered that the decision in *Northampton Theatre Trust*, is very relevant to claims for the repayment of VAT accounted for on temporary memberships in the period 5th December 1996 to the beginning of the three year period ending on the date of the claim.

According to HMRC, a decision from the ECJ is not likely to be received until mid 2013 at the earliest. They have also set out their grounds for appealing the decision in *Bridport &*

MATCH PLAY – FINAL ROUND

West Dorset Golf Club in Revenue & Customs Brief 30/11 which is reproduced in Appendix B.

CHAPTER 12: A VISIT FROM THE ROYAL AND ANCIENT GOLF CLUB

How to deal with a VAT inspection

The R&A, as it is more commonly known, equates with HMRC in that it is the body responsible for enforcing the rules of golf (c.f. VAT), and they both play a large part in the setting of the relevant legislation.

It is therefore important that when an HMRC Officer visits the club, he is accorded the same treatment as would a visitor from the R&A. At the very least he should be met by the Secretary and Treasurer and, with the possible exception of the Captain, no one else should be responsible for dealing with any enquiry. The Club Officers should be absolutely sure that they understand what the HMRC Officer requires, and that they are familiar with the basic rules of VAT as far as golf clubs are concerned.

Generally speaking, provided that there are adequate controls on cash collection e.g. bar takings and gaming machine takings, and that the liability of supplies made (income received) is correct, then the recovery of input tax is the area where the Officer is likely to spend most time.

On the assumption that returns have been submitted regularly and on time, and that the partial exemption calculations and annual adjustment are in order, a golf club is unlikely to receive a visit in the current economic climate based on normal day-to-day trading except on rare occasions. Problems do arise, however, when major clubhouse or course expenditure takes place. Major deviations from the norm in the statistical values in Boxes 6 and 7 of the return are sufficient to jolt the HMRC computer into life resulting in an immediate visit and, if all is not well, an assessment for the Officer is effectively handed to him on a plate.

It is rare for a club to construct a completely new clubhouse, but if they do, and it costs in excess of £250,000 (this is not meant to be a joke!) the Capital Goods Scheme (CGS) applies because the building is used for both taxable and exempt purposes. However, the scheme also applies to an extension of a clubhouse where the value of the extension exceeds £250,000 and the floor area is increased by 10% or more. How many golf club treasurers/secretaries are aware even of the existence of these rules, never mind how they should be applied? To be fair, it will not be a common occurrence for such major works to be undertaken and it is to be hoped that professional advice would be taken from the club's accountants, or a VAT specialist, as appropriate, before any contracts are signed or building work commences. I would even argue that the advice should be taken *before* planning permission is requested. The principle of the CGS is that the initial deduction of input tax is based on the previous year's partial exemption taxable percentage. For the next nine years the amount of input tax claimed in that first year is adjusted, not by the partial exemption figure, but by the *actual taxable use of the building* which may be substantially different depending on how the figure is calculated. The application of the CGS warrants a book in its own right and is clearly beyond the scope of this work, but the visit by the HMRC Officer is not!

One of the biggest causes of problems on inspection visits is the wish of the responsible person(s) to please the visiting Officer by answering each question on the basis of the "answer the Officer wants to hear". This is a most dangerous attitude and can only lead to trouble. Answer questions truthfully, and if you don't know the answer, agree to provide it in writing later, or suggest that the Officer contacts your accountant for the answer. Don't try to be clever and don't tell lies – it doesn't pay.

As visits to your club will only be made infrequently, it is unlikely that the visiting Officer will have visited the course before. If that is the case, give him a conducted tour of the premises before he asks. Bearing in mind the words of caution emphasised in the preceding chapters, explain how the bar and catering services are provided, and cash is accounted for. Introduce him to the golf professional, let him meet the head green-keeper (he probably spends more of the club's money than anyone else), and, of course, always offer hospitality of tea and coffee. Be careful about this – a slap-up lunch might just be taken as attempted bribery – HMRC Officials do have their own rules about what they can or cannot accept, but a plate of biscuits with the coffee will usually be accepted in good grace. If the visit is interesting and pleasant for the Officer, there is less chance that he will be argumentative and difficult over minor matters in return. Obviously, if something is wrong, he has a duty to make sure that it is corrected.

If your VAT returns are prepared by an accountant outside the club, make sure that the legally required VAT accounts and working papers are made available at the start of the visit. HMRC's current practice is to send a letter in advance of the visit setting out what accounting and other records are required. If they are all ready and waiting, in good order, the Officer will be impressed and you are less likely to be subjected to an extended visit.

Finally, remember that VAT Officers are human beings who eat, drink and sleep like the rest of us. It is just possible that your visitor might play golf or has been a guest at your club. Make sure that if this is the case, this fact is turned to your advantage.

CONCLUSION

As forecast in the first edition of this book, the EU legislation, namely Articles 13A(1)(m) and 13A(2) of the EC Sixth Directive, has finally come before the UK Courts and the ECJ with resounding defeats for the British Government. The fact that the House of Lords finally came to the view that the UK Government had acted illegally in not setting a reasonable transition period for the imposition of the three-year rule is an added bonus for members' golf clubs.

It would be foolish to think, however, that HM Revenue & Customs will take the *Canterbury Hockey Clubs* decision lying down. Claims for a refund of VAT accounted for on temporary memberships have been rejected at the first hurdle, and it may well be that protracted legal argument will be necessary before common sense prevails. Members' clubs should therefore take their own legal advice about any claim they could make but the fact that the 31st March 2009 deadline in BN 78 has passed, does not prevent claims being made as set out in Chapter 10, page 38.

On the other side of the coin, several private clubs have failed miserably in trying to set up a "not for profit golf club" within a profit-making environment. The anti-avoidance legislation is tightly drawn, but I have no doubt that there will be further attempts to overcome these difficulties in the future.

Finally, can I wish all those who read this book, the very best in golf. I have been lucky in that I have enjoyed all sports from my earliest school days, and been able to take advantage of the opportunities that have come my way. The

CONCLUSION

serious groin injury that made me give up bowling fast on the cricket field resulted in golf becoming a serious obsession. If early retirement has resulted in the writing of this book and a reduction in my handicap – what more could I ask from life?

"Real golfers go to work to relax"

George Dillon

APPENDIX A: Legislation Extracts

EC Sixth Directive, Article 13

Exemptions within the territory of the country

A. Exemptions for certain activities in the public interest

1. Without prejudice to other Community provisions, Member States shall exempt the following under conditions which they shall lay down for the purpose of ensuring the correct and straightforward application of such exemptions and of preventing any possible evasion, avoidance or abuse:...

    (m) certain services closely linked to sport or physical education supplied by non-profit-making organisations to persons taking part in sport or physical education....

2. (a) Member States may make the granting to bodies other than those governed by public law of each exemption provided for in 1(b),(g),(h),(i),(l),(m) and (n) of this Article subject in each individual case to one or more of the following conditions
    - they shall not systematically aim to make a profit, but any profits nevertheless arising shall not be distributed, but shall be assigned to the continuance or improvement of the service supplied,
    - they shall be managed and administered on an essentially voluntary basis by persons who have no direct or indirect interest, either themselves or through intermediaries, in the results of the activities concerned,
    - they shall charge prices approved by the public authorities or which do not exceed such approved prices or, in respect of those services not subject to approval, prices lower than those charged for similar services by commercial enterprises subject to value added tax,
    - exemption of the services concerned shall not be likely to create distortions of competition such as to place at a disadvantage commercial enterprises liable to value added tax.

APPENDIX A

(b) The supply of services or goods shall not be granted exemption as provided for in 1(b),(g),(h),(i),(l),(m) and (n) above if:
- it is not essential to the transactions exempted,
- its basic purpose is to obtain additional income for the organisation by carrying out transactions which are in direct competition with those of commercial enterprises liable for value added tax.

This legislation has now been repealed and incorporated into Council Directive 112/2006, Articles 132 and 133 without material amendment.

VATA 1994

Schedule 9, Group 10

Item No.	Sport, sports competitions and physical education
1.	The grant of a right to enter a competition in sport or physical recreation where the consideration for the grant consists in money which is to be allocated wholly towards the provision of a prize or prizes awarded in that competition.
2.	The grant, by a non-profit-making body established for the purposes of sport or physical recreation, of a right to enter a competition in such an activity.
3.	The supply by a non-profit making body to an individual, except, where the body operates a membership scheme, an individual who is not a member, of services closely linked with and essential to sport or physical education in which the individual is taking part.
Notes:	(1) Item 3 does not include the supply of any services by a non-profit making body of residential accommodation, catering or transport.
	(2) An individual shall only be considered to be a member of a non-profit making body for the purpose of Item 3 where he is granted membership for a period of three

months or more.

(3) In Item 3 a "non-profit making body" does not include—
   (a) a local authority;
   (b) a Government department within the meaning of section 41(6); or
   (c) a non-departmental public body which is listed in the 1993 edition of the publication prepared by the Office of Public Service and Science and known as Public Bodies.

[(4) For the purposes of this Group a body shall be taken, in relation to a sports supply, to be subject to commercial influence if, and only if, there is a time in the relevant period when—
   (a) a relevant supply was made to that body by a person associated with it at that time;
   (b) an emolument was paid by that body to such a person;
   (c) an agreement existed for either or both of the following to take place after the end of that period, namely—
      (i) the making of a relevant supply to that body by such a person; or
      (ii) the payment by that body to such a person of any emoluments.

(5) In this Group "the relevant period", in relation to a sports supply, means—
   (a) where that supply is one made before 1 January 2003, the period beginning with 14 January 1999 and ending with the making of that sports supply; and
   (b) where that supply is one made on or after 1 January 2003, the period of three years ending with the making of that sports supply.

(6) Subject to Note (7), in this Group "relevant supply", in relation to any body, means a supply falling within any of the following paragraphs—
   (a) the grant of any interest in or right over land which at

APPENDIX A

any time in the relevant period was or was expected to become sports land;
(b) the grant of any licence to occupy any land which at any such time was or was expected to become sports land;
(c) the grant, in the case of land in Scotland, of any personal right to call for or be granted any such interest or right as is mentioned in paragraph (a) above;
(d) a supply arising from a grant falling within paragraph (a), (b) or (c) above, other than a grant made before 1 April 1996;
(e) the supply of any services consisting in the management or administration of any facilities provided by that body;
(f) the supply of any goods or services for a consideration in excess of what would have been agreed between parties entering into a commercial transaction at arm's length.

(7) A supply which has been, or is to be or may be, made by any person shall not be taken, in relation to a sports supply made by any body, to be a relevant supply for the purposes of this Group if—
(a) the principal purpose of that body is confined, at the time when the sports supply is made, to the provision for employees of that person of facilities for use for or in connection with sport or physical recreation, or both;
(b) the supply in question is one made by a charity or local authority or one which (if it is made) will be made by a person who is a charity or local authority at the time when the sports supply is made;
(c) the supply in question is a grant falling within Note (6)(a) to (c) which has been made, or (if it is made) will be made, for a nominal consideration;
(d) the supply in question is one arising from such a grant as is mentioned in paragraph (c) above and is not itself a supply the consideration for which was, or will

or may be, more than a nominal consideration; or
(e) the supply in question—
  (i) is a grant falling within Note (6)(a) to (c) which is made for no consideration; but
  (ii) falls to be treated as a supply of goods or services, or (if it is made) will fall to be so treated, by reason only of the application, in accordance with paragraph 9 of Schedule 4, of paragraph 5 of that Schedule.

(8) Subject to Note (10), a person shall be taken, for the purposes of this Group, to have been associated with a body at any of the following times, that is to say—
  (a) the time when a supply was made to that body by that person;
  (b) the time when an emolument was paid by that body to that person; or
  (c) the time when an agreement was in existence for the making of a relevant supply or the payment of emoluments,
  if, at that time, or at another time (whether before or after that time) in the relevant period, that person was an officer or shadow officer of that body or an intermediary for supplies to that body.

(9) Subject to Note (10), a person shall also be taken, for the purposes of this Group, to have been associated with a body at a time mentioned in paragraph (a), (b) or (c) of Note (8) if, at that time, he was connected with another person who in accordance with that Note—
  (a) is to be taken to have been so associated at that time; or
  (b) would be taken to have been so associated were that time the time of a supply by the other person to that body.

(10) Subject to Note (11), a person shall not be taken for the purposes of this Group to have been associated with a body at a time mentioned in paragraph (a), (b) or (c) of Note (8) if the only times in the relevant period when

APPENDIX A

that person or the person connected with him was an officer or shadow officer of the body are times before 1 January 2000.

(11) Note (10) does not apply where (but for that Note) the body would be treated as subject to commercial influence at any time in the relevant period by virtue of—
   (a) the existence of any agreement entered into on or after 14 January 1999 and before 1 January 2000; or
   (b) anything done in pursuance of any such agreement.

(12) For the purposes of this Group a person shall be taken, in relation to a sports supply, to have been at all times in the relevant period an intermediary for supplies to the body making that supply if—
   (a) at any time in that period either a supply was made to him by another person or an agreement for the making of a supply to him by another was in existence; and
   (b) the circumstances were such that, if—
      (i) that body had been the person to whom the supply was made or (in the case of an agreement) the person to whom it was to be or might be made; and
      (ii) Note (7) above were to be disregarded to the extent (if at all) that it would prevent the supply from being a relevant supply, the body would have fallen to be regarded in relation to the sports supply as subject to commercial influence.

(13) In determining for the purposes of Note (12) or this Note whether there are such circumstances as are mentioned in paragraph (b) of that Note in the case of any supply, that Note and this Note shall be applied first for determining whether the person by whom the supply was made, or was to be or might be made, was himself an intermediary for supplies to the body in question, and so on through any number of other supplies or agreements.

(14) In determining for the purposes of this Group whether a supply made by any person was made by an intermediary for supplies to a body, it shall be immaterial that the supply by that person was made before the making of the supply or agreement by reference to which that person falls to be regarded as such an intermediary.

(15) Without prejudice to the generality of subsection (1AA) of section 43, for the purpose of determining—
   (a) whether a relevant supply has at any time been made to any person;
   (b) whether there has at any time been an agreement for the making of a relevant supply to any person; and
   (c) whether a person falls to be treated as an intermediary for the supplies to any body by reference to supplies that have been, were to be or might have been made to him,

references in the preceding Notes to a supply shall be deemed to include references to a supply falling for other purposes to be disregarded in accordance with section 43(1)(a).

(16) In this Group—

"agreement" includes any arrangement or understanding (whether or not legally enforceable);

"emolument" means any emolument (within the meaning of the Income Tax Acts) the amount of which falls or may fall, in accordance with the agreement under which it is payable, to be determined or varied wholly or partly by reference—
   (i) to the profits from some or all of the activities of the body paying the emolument; or
   (ii) to the level of that body's gross income from some or all of its activities;

"employees", in relation to a person, includes retired employees of that person;

APPENDIX A

"grant" includes an assignment or surrender;

"officer", in relation to a body, includes—
  (i) a director of a body corporate; and
  (ii) any committee member or trustee concerned in the general control and management of the administration of the body;

"shadow officer", in relation to a body, means a person in accordance with whose directions or instructions the members or officers of the body are accustomed to act;

"sports land", in relation to any body, means any land used or held for use for or in connection with the provision by that body of facilities for use for or in connection with sport or physical recreation, or both;

"sports supply" means a supply which, if made by an eligible body, would fall within Item 2 or 3.

(17) For the purposes of this Group any question whether a person is connected with another shall be determined in accordance with section 839 of the Taxes Act (connected persons).]

Income and Corporation Taxes Act 1988 s. 839.

(1) For the purposes of, and subject to, the provisions of the Tax Acts which apply this section, any question whether a person is connected with another shall be determined in accordance with the following provisions of this section (any provision that one person is connected with another being taken to mean that they are connected with one another).

(2) A person is connected with an individual if that person is the individual's wife or husband, or is a relative, or the wife or husband of a relative, of the individual or of the individual's wife or husband.

[(3) A person, in his capacity as trustee of a settlement, is connected with—
  (a) any individual who in relation to the settlement is a settlor,
  (b) any person who is connected with such an individual, and
  (c) any body corporate which is connected with that settlement.

In this subsection "settlement" and "settlor" have the same meaning as in [Chapter 5 of Part 5 of ITTOIA 2005 (see section 620 of that Act)].]

[(3A) For the purpose of subsection (3) above a body corporate is connected with a settlement if—
  (a) it is a close company (or only not a close company because it is not resident in the United Kingdom) and the participators include the trustees of the settlement; or
  (b) it is controlled (within the meaning of section 840) by a company falling within paragraph (a) above.]

(4) Except in relation to acquisitions or disposals of partnership assets pursuant to bona fide commercial arrangements, a person is connected with any person with whom he is in partnership, and with the wife or husband or relative of any individual with whom he is in partnership.

(5) A company is connected with another company—
  (a) if the same person has control of both, or a person has control of one and persons connected with him, or he and persons connected with him, have control of the other; or

APPENDIX A

    (b) if a group of two or more persons has control of each company, and the groups either consist of the same persons or could be regarded as consisting of the same persons by treating (in one or more cases) a member of either group as replaced by a person with whom he is connected.

(6) A company is connected with another person if that person has control of it or if that person and persons connected with him together have control of it.

(7) Any two or more persons acting together to secure or exercise control of a company shall be treated in relation to that company as connected with one another and with any person acting on the directions of any of them to secure or exercise control of the company.

(8) In this section—

"company" includes any body corporate or unincorporated association, but does not include a partnership, and this section shall apply in relation to any unit trust scheme as if the scheme were a company and as if the rights of the unit holders were shares in the company;

"control" shall be construed in accordance with section 416; and

"relative" means brother, sister, ancestor or lineal descendant.

APPENDIX B: HMRC notices

Customs & Excise Business Brief 3/96

16 February 1996. Business Brief 3/96

VAT exemption of non-profit making sports centres

Following a recent VAT tribunal case Customs and Excise are clarifying the VAT exemption for sporting services provided by non-profit making sports centres.

Exemption from VAT of certain sporting and physical education services supplied by non-profit making bodies was introduced on 1 April 1994, although in practice such bodies could backdate the exemption and claim a refund of VAT covering the period 1 January 1990 – 31 March 1994, if they wished.

Under the terms of the exemption a non-profit making body operating a membership scheme has to tax at the standard rate all services supplied to non-members. However any such body, which is not operating a membership scheme, has to exempt sporting and physical education services supplied to all individual participants, for example, where usage is entirely on a pay and play basis.

In considering the appeal by the *Basingstoke and District Sports Trust Ltd v C & E Commrs. [1995] VATDR 405* against refusal by Customs and Excise of VAT exemption for non-members, the VAT tribunal decided that the privilege cards, issued by the Trust and previously described as membership cards, did not amount to a membership scheme for the purposes of exemption. Consequently supplies by the Trust of qualifying services to all users of the Trust's sporting and physical recreation facilities (not just privilege card holders) are exempt from VAT.

In the light of the tribunal decision and following discussion within sports representative bodies, Customs and Excise have

APPENDIX B

issued the following clarification of the applicability of the exemption to sports centres operated by charitable trusts and like bodies—

"Where a sports centre operated by a charitable trust or similar non-profit making body makes supplies of sporting and physical education services of a type which would normally qualify for exemption from VAT (see para.18 of Notice No 701/45/94 'Sport and physical education') and does not operate a full membership scheme (for example where members do not have voting rights or any form of control over the management of the centre), such services will be exempt from VAT. This relates only to supplies to individuals or groups of individuals using the centre and applies irrespective of whether users are called 'members' for the purposes of obtaining discount on use of the facilities."

Where such a sports centre operates a full membership scheme and limits its application to selected activities or locations, exemption of qualifying services will be limited to supplies to members, even if an activity is not used by members. For example where a centre provides a swimming pool and squash courts and the membership scheme is only for squash players, supplies to all users of the swimming pool, other than squash members, will continue to be standard-rated.

The position of sports centres operated by local and other public authorities, which are specifically excluded from exemption by VATA 1994 Sch.9 Group 10 item 3 note 3 is unaffected by this statement.

Sports centres whose supplies are affected by this clarification or who wish to take advantage of the repayment arrangements detailed in Annex A to Notice No 701/45/94 or require further information should contact their local VAT business advice centre listed under Customs and Excise in the telephone book.

HM Revenue & Customs Budget Notice BN 78 dated 12th March 2008

VAT: *transitional period for claims*

Who is likely to be affected?

1. Businesses registered for VAT between 1 April 1973 and 1 May 1997 who either declared more output VAT than they were liable for, or claimed less input VAT than entitled to.

General description of the measure

2. Legislation will be introduced in Finance Bill 2008 to provide a transitional period to 31 March 2009, during which eligible businesses can make VAT claims for rights that accrued before the introduction in 1996 and 1997 of the three-year time limit for claims.

3. The legislation will also correspondingly amend the powers of assessment of HM Revenue & Customs (HMRC) to ensure that assessments may be made to recover any amounts paid, which are subsequently found to have been incorrectly claimed by business.

Operative date

4. The transitional period will run to 31 March 2009.

Current law and proposed revisions

Regulation 29(1A) of the Value Added Tax Regulations 1995

5. Regulation 29(1A) provides that no claim for input tax can be made more than three years after the due date of the return, for the accounting period in which the input tax was incurred.

6. In January 2008, the House of Lords held in its judgments in *Michael Fleming (trading as Bodycraft)* and *Condé Nast Publications Ltd* that, because there was no transitional period when the three-year cap was first introduced, the three-year

APPENDIX B

time limit does not have effect for any right to claim input tax that accrued before it was enacted on 1 May 1997 until an adequate transitional period has been provided.

7. This measure will give effect to the judgment of the House of Lords by providing a transitional period during which claims for input tax can be made, for accounting periods ending between 1 April 1973 and 1 May 1997, before they become subject to the three-year time limit.

Section 80(4) of the Value Added Tax Act 1994

8. Section 80 provides that where a person accounts for more output VAT than is due, they can claim it back from HMRC. Section 80(4) provides that HMRC are not liable to pay any claim made more than three years after the end of the accounting period to which it relates.

9. HMRC considers that the House of Lords' judgments in *Michael Fleming (trading as Bodycraft)* and *Condé Nast Publications Ltd* also apply to rights to claim overpaid output tax that accrued before the three-year time limit was enacted on 4 December 1996 until an adequate transitional period has been provided.

10. This measure will provide a transitional period during which claims for overdeclared output tax can be made, for accounting periods ending between 1 April 1973 and 4 December 1996, before they become subject to the three-year time limit.

Section 80(4A) of the Value Added Tax Act 1994

11. Assessments to recover amounts incorrectly paid by HMRC to businesses who claim under section 80 must be made within two years of HMRC having acquired evidence of facts, sufficient to justify the making of the assessment.

12. This measure will add a two-year time limit from the end of the accounting period in which an erroneous payment is

made. This will ensure that HMRC are able recover amounts paid out where it is later discovered repayment was mistaken.

13. This will also bring these assessment time limits into line with those for HMRC's other VAT assessment powers.

Section 73(2) of the Value Added Tax Act 1994

14. Assessments to recover amounts incorrectly paid by HMRC to businesses on input tax claims must be made within two years of the end of the accounting period in which the claim is made.

15. This measure will amend the time limit, so that it runs from the end of the accounting period in which the claim was paid, ensuring that HMRC will be able to recover any amounts incorrectly paid.

Further advice

16. If you have any questions about this change, please contact Pauline Walsh on 0113 389 4432 (e-mail: pauline.walsh3@hmrc.gsi.gov.uk). Information about Budget measures is available on the HM Revenue & Customs website at www.hmrc.gov.uk

APPENDIX B

Revenue & Customs Brief 30/11

VAT: HMRC's position following the First-Tier Tribunal decision in the case of The Bridport and West Dorset Golf Club Limited

This brief explains HM Revenue & Customs' (HMRC's) position following the First-Tier Tribunal decision in the case of The *Bridport and West Dorset Golf Club case (TC/2009/122260)*. The appeal concerned the VAT liability of green fees charged by the golf club to non-members.

Background

Bridport and West Dorset Golf Club is a non-profit making members' golf club. The issue before the tribunal was whether the charges, known as green fees, made by the club to visiting non-members in return for the right to play golf are exempt from VAT or, as HMRC maintained, standard rated.

Under VATA 1994 Schedule 9 Group 10 Item 3, supplies by non-profit making bodies of services closely linked and essential to sport to individuals taking part in sport are exempt from VAT. However, where the body operates a membership scheme, any supplies to individuals who are not members are excluded from the exemption and subject to VAT.

The tribunal concluded that by restricting the exemption to supplies made to members, the UK law was acting contrary to the purpose of the exemption in the Principal VAT Directive (or, in other words, had failed to "correctly implement its terms"). It was not persuaded by HMRC's argument that the exclusion applied to non-members was justified on grounds that it reduced distortion of competition. As a result, it agreed with the golf club that supplies to non-members of green fees were exempt from VAT.

HMRC's position

HMRC believes that the tribunal has erred in interpreting EU law and remains of the view that where clubs that run membership schemes make charges to non-members for the use of certain sporting facilities, such as green fees, the charges are standard rated. They have, as a result, sought permission to appeal to the Upper Tier Tribunal.

Decisions of the First-Tier Tribunal are binding only on the parties to the decision. Consequently, we do not propose to pay other claims already submitted and we are not inviting new claims in the wake of this decision. Any claims that are submitted will be rejected.

HMRC consider that businesses should continue to follow the guidance in Notice 701/45 Sport and standard-rate these types of supplies made to non-members of a membership club. Should any golf clubs decide to exempt their green fees on the basis of the First-Tier Tribunal's decision, HMRC will assess the underdeclared tax and enforce the assessments. Penalties may also be applicable in such cases.

Issued 27 July 2011

APPENDIX C: Golf Club VAT cases

The intention of this book is to provide advice on the application of VAT to members' golf clubs based on the extant legislation at January 2013. The list of VAT and Duties Tribunals and Court cases only includes those which are relevant at publication date.

EU Legislation

Keswick Golf Club and others v. Commissioners of Customs & Excise (No 15493) 24 February 1998

The appeal was against a written decision of Customs & Excise, that the payment of green fees by temporary members were liable to VAT at the standard rate.

The grounds for the appeal were that the income should be treated as exempt under the provisions of the EC Sixth Directive, Article 13(A)(1)(m).

The arguments in support of this contention were that Article 13(A)(2)(a) states that

"Member States may make the granting of exemption to bodies…. subject to one or more of the following conditions….

- exemption of the services concerned shall not be likely to create distortions of competition such as to place at a disadvantage commercial enterprises liable to value added tax."

and

"the supply of goods and services shall not be granted exemption….if

- **it is not essential to the transactions exempted**

- **its basic purpose is to obtain additional income for the organisation by carrying out transactions which are in direct competition with those of commercial enterprises liable for value added tax."**

and that Keswick Golf Club did not place at a commercial disadvantage commercial enterprises, and would not obtain additional income as a result of the exemption being granted.

In the end, the Tribunal Chairman openly disregarded the evidence heard as he believed that it was not a deciding factor, and ruled that the UK was entitled to legislate that green fees (temporary memberships) should be standard rated, and dismissed the appeal. The club involved considered taking the matter to a higher court but decided, in the end, that the costs of so doing were higher than they could afford to risk. Although the club received support in the form of articles written in professional journals following the decision, no other club has considered it worthwhile to make another attempt to overturn this decision.

Kennemer Golf & Country Club v. Staatssecretaris van Financien (Case C-174/00) 21 March 2002 (European Court of Justice)

The golf club derived its income from members' subscriptions and admission fees and from day subscription fees paid by non-members. For several years the golf club made an operating surplus which was placed in a reserve account for non-annual expenditure. The club's VAT return did not include tax on the fees from non-members on the grounds that its services to non-members were exempt under Netherlands legislation implementing EC Sixth Directive, Article 13A(1)(m) and the first indent of Article 13A(2)(a).

The Netherlands tax authorities considered that the club was aiming to make a profit on its services to non-members. The matter was referred to the ECJ for a preliminary ruling on the correct interpretation of the relevant legislation.

It was held

(1) Article 13A(1)(m) was to be interpreted as meaning that the categorisation of an organisation as non-profit making had to be based on all the organisations activities.

(2) An organisation might be categorised as non-profit making even if it systematically sought to achieve surpluses which it then used for the purposes of the provision of its services.

(3) Article 2(1) was to be interpreted as meaning that the annual subscription fees of members of such a sports association could constitute the consideration for the services provided by the association, even though members who did not use, or did not regularly use, the association's facilities, still had to pay their annual subscription fees.

Canterbury Hockey Club and Canterbury Ladies Hockey Club v. The Commissioners for HM Revenue and Customs

The High Court made a reference to the ECJ for a preliminary ruling made in the High Court on 29 May 2007. The reference related to the interpretation of Article 13A(1)(m) of the EC Sixth Directive. It was agreed by all parties that the clubs were members' only sports clubs which fielded a number of hockey teams. The clubs are unincorporated associations without legal personality.

The dispute concerned the VAT liability of affiliation fees to England Hockey. HM Revenue & Customs maintained that they were standard-rated whereas the Hockey Clubs contended that they were exempt under Article 13A(1)(m). The Hockey Clubs appealed against that decision and the VAT & Duties Tribunal held that the services supplied by England Hockey could be treated as supplies made to the individual members of the Hockey Clubs. The Commissioners appealed that decision to the High Court who referred the matter to the ECJ for a ruling on the meaning of "persons" in Article 13A(1)(m).

In a comprehensive decision, the Court went further than simply answering the questions asked and established the following two points:

1. **Article 13A(1)(m) of the Sixth Council Directive 77/388/EEC of 17th May 1977 on the harmonisation of the laws of the Member States relating to turnover taxes – Common system of value added tax: uniform basis of assessment is to be interpreted as meaning that, in the context of persons taking part in sport, it includes services supplied to corporate persons and to unincorporated associations, provided that – which it is for the national court to establish – those services are closely linked and essential to sport, that they are supplied by non-profit-making organisations and that their true beneficiaries are persons taking part in sport.**

2. **The expression "certain services closely linked to sport", in Article 13A(1)(m) of the Sixth Directive 77/388, does not**

allow the Member States to limit the exemption under that provision to the recipients of the services in question.

Whether or not a non-profit making body

De Vere Golf and Leisure Ltd and De Vere Group plc (No 18078) 8 April 2003

The first appellant appealed against
(1) a decision contained in a letter from Customs & Excise that the first appellant was not a "non-profit making body" with the result that supplies relating to sport made by the first appellant were standard-rated and not exempt supplies;
(2) an assessment of £8.7 million including interest;
(3) an additional assessment in the sum of £277,642; and
(4) a serious misdeclaration penalty in the sum of £1.187 million.

In its decision, the Tribunal stated that

"The purpose of the value added tax exemption is for organisations acting in the public interest and whose activities are directed to non-commercial purposes. We do not consider that the first appellant was an organisation acting in the public interest and we think that it and the group had commercial purposes, as the aim of the group was to achieve profits for its members….and in the light of all the facts of this case, we do not consider that the first appellant satisfies the requirements enabling it to be categorised as non-profit making.

and

APPENDIX C

The whole commercial enterprise of the group is clearly profitable and the leisure enterprises are firmly embedded in it."

The appeal on the first issue was dismissed with the parties being given the right to return to the Tribunal if agreement could not be reached on the assessments.

Chobham Golf Club v. Commissioners of Customs & Excise (No 14867) 26 March 1997

Chobham Golf Club appealed against a decision of Customs & Excise to the effect that the club was not a non-profit making body and that the supplies of sporting services it made to its members were therefore not exempt supplies.

The club was originally a proprietary club in the ownership of the Compton Holdings group. The group found itself in financial difficulties and disposed of the club to a group of companies in which the current Secretary, at the material time, had a major interest. As well as the club, there was a group of companies consisting of Chobham Golf Club Ltd. (the landlord company), and Chobham Golf Club Management Ltd. (the management company).

In its decision, the Tribunal came to the view that there was no profit seeking purpose or intention or motive. Once the rent was paid, the management fees paid, the bank paid the interest due, and normal creditors paid, the surplus can be disposed of in any way the club thinks fit – other than by distribution to members. There was no evidence to suggest that any such surplus would find its way into the hands of the Secretary or his associates, and the appeal was allowed.

This decision was clearly based on the particular facts of the case but in view of the commercial influence rules at Note 4 to Group 10 of Schedule 9, great care must be taken if Chobham is to be relied upon in another appeal.

Recovery of input tax

Burntisland Golf House Club v. Commissioners of Customs & Excise (No 6340) 12 August 1991

The golf course and clubhouse were owned by Burntisland Golf Company Ltd. The trustees owned 70% of the shares in the company with 30% being held by members of the appellant club. The club leased the course and clubhouse for 21 years from 1966 but the lease has continued since its expiry. The club was responsible for all repair work and upkeep both internal and external. The club was debarred from making any alterations without the permission of the trustees, and all alterations executed, fixtures and fittings introduced by the tenants, so far as they could not be removed, belonged to the proprietors without payment.

The club recovered input tax in respect of alterations to the clubhouse approved by the trustees, which the respondents subsequently assessed on the basis that the work was done for the benefit of the company.

The Tribunal distinguished supplies made for the benefit of the business and those made for the purpose of the business. It decided on the facts that the supplies were made both for the purpose and the benefit of the club and its members, and allowed the appeal, notwithstanding that, on termination of the lease, the company would benefit from the said alterations.

APPENDIX C

Milnathort Golf Club v. Commissioners of Customs & Excise (No 17889) 11 November 2002

Planning approval was granted for major alterations and upgrades to the course and clubhouse. A lottery grant was approved which specifically excluded the lounge, dining area, bar kitchen and store. Tenders were received for the work, which were accepted.

At the completion of the works a composite bill was rendered by, and paid to, each of the contractors. No detail was provided on the invoices from any of the contractors but shortly thereafter they were asked to specify which parts of their work were attributable to the bar (non lottery grant) area. In the end, the information was supplied although in one case, it was based on the tender price rather than what had actually been provided. The appellants reclaimed input tax in the amounts disclosed as appropriate. After examination of the accounts, the respondents declined to accept that input tax had been properly reclaimed and made an assessment on the basis that there was a single supply which should be treated as residual input tax and apportioned using the partial exemption standard method.

In the end, the Tribunal was satisfied that the initial rendering and payment of the single figure accounts for the whole works done by the contractors was not fatal to an attribution of the work to taxable and non-taxable areas. The evidence before the Tribunal was that the work was done and that it could be attributed accordingly, and the appeal was allowed, and the assessment discharged.

Elsham Golf Club Ltd. v. Commissioners of Customs & Excise (No 18107) 28 April 2003

In its decision, the Tribunal had to decide whether the club was entitled to full recovery of input tax incurred on works to the clubhouse providing a new restaurant/dining room extension. In particular, whether the restaurant was used "exclusively" for the purpose of making taxable supplies. The Tribunal found that the restaurant was used by the club, albeit rarely, both for holding meetings and for fundraising events. Both are exempt supplies and the appeal was dismissed.

This is a very important decision of which all clubs should be aware. During the pre-tribunal negotiations with Customs, they offered the club a special partial exemption method based on "sectors" of the clubhouse and course. This was turned down by the club and thus the assessment based on the standard method was upheld when the special method would have produced a lower figure. There is also an argument that a fundraising event, where, presumably, an entry fee was charged, is a taxable supply, not exempt.

If a members' meeting was held there would be no income attributable to it and it is doubtful whether the argument, that an exempt supply has been made, can be justified. It is more likely that, at that time, members would be consuming drinks purchased in the bar and standard rated supplies were being made.

APPENDIX C

VAT liability of income

Copthorne Village Golf Club v. Commissioners of Customs & Excise (No 17426) 5 October 2001

In a case where the circumstances are rather unusual, Copthorne Golf Club (the main club) owned and ran a members' golf club. For reasons that are shrouded in local history, a second golf club, Copthorne Village Golf Club, was allowed to use the course of the main club under a licence granted to them. The licence did not extend to the use of the clubhouse. The annual consideration for the right was calculated as a proportion of the main club's costs in the preceding financial year.

The appellants maintained that the licence fee should be exempt from VAT. The village club was not registered for VAT.

The Tribunal ruled that the licence was not exempt as a licence to occupy land under VATA 1994, Schedule 9, Group 1, Item 1, neither was it an exempt supply under Item 3 to Group 10 of Schedule 9 of the Act. The supplies that were being made under the licence were not to individuals, but to an unincorporated association comprised of individuals. The supplies had to be construed strictly, and the members of the village club were not members of "the eligible body", namely the main club. The appeal was therefore dismissed by the Tribunal but with an expressed hope that the two clubs might be able to find some way of joining that would overcome the VAT problem but would not destroy the historical origins of the village club.

GOLF CLUB CASES

Abbotsley Golf and Squash Club Ltd v. Commissioners of Customs & Excise (No 15042) 2 May 1997

The club appealed against a written decision of the Commissioners that a fee received by the appellant for the grant of a license to the Abbotsley Country Club Ltd was a standard rated supply on which VAT was due.

The Tribunal decided that, in the first part, that there was a supply of a licence granted to Abbotsley Country Club Ltd. In the second part, a licence to occupy land would not suffice for exemption from standard rating if it was "the grant of facilities for playing any sport or participating in any physical recreation". The appellant stated that it had granted no such facilities. It had given a simple licence to occupy land. The purpose was occupation for use as a golf course and club, but that the grant itself contained no such facilities.

The Tribunal, in its conclusion, decided that there was a licence to occupy land entered into under the provisions of the VATA 1994, Schedule 9, Group 1, Item 1, the exclusion from exemption in item 1(m) having no application.

Different classes of membership

West Essex Golf Club v. Commissioners of Customs & Excise (No 7321) 28 February 1992

This appeal concerned the question of what is the value of the supply of services by a golf club to its members in a situation where the club has two levels of subscription for each class of member. The standard subscription is paid by the member who has made a loan to the club (a "noteholder"); a higher subscription is payable by a member who is a "non-noteholder". The Commissioners gave a ruling that

"the value of the facilities of membership supplied to noteholders is to be determined by reference to the full fees charged to non-noteholders."

In its decision, the Tribunal followed the decision in *Exeter Golf and Country Club* [1981] STC 211 (Court of Appeal). The consideration for the supply had to be a subjective value – the consideration actually received minus the open market value. This was confirmed as the subscription paid plus interest that would have been earned on the investment in the open market.

Miscellaneous

Tall Pines Golf and Leisure Co. Ltd v. Commissioners of Customs & Excise (No 16538) 3 March 2000

The owner of Tall Pines Golf Club, the grantor, was advised by a large firm of Chartered Accountants to enter into a scheme to take advantage of the "sporting exemption" for eligible bodies. The scheme involved the grantor entering into three agreements with Tall Pines Golf Club Ltd ("the Operator"), namely,

(1) An agreement for the transfer of part of its business

(2) An agreement for the provision of banking services

(3) A non-exclusive turnover licence

The Tribunal decided that the agreement for banking services was immaterial to the VAT issue at stake.

The scheme was, by its very nature, complex and the detail goes well beyond the parameters of this book, suffice to say that the Tribunal decided that Tall Pines Golf and Leisure Co. Ltd made one principal service, namely a supply of a fully equipped golf course, and that the supplies of the name Tall Pines Golf Club, and the equipment, were ancillary to the principal service, and the appeal was dismissed.

Whilst not in any way criticising advice on tax avoidance given by reputable Chartered Accountants and VAT Specialists, however plausible it may be, one cannot guarantee that the VAT and Duties Tribunal or the Courts will accept it. The words of the Tribunal Chairman in the appeal by *De Vere Golf and Leisure Ltd.*, referred to earlier in this chapter, should never be forgotten -

"the purpose of the value added tax exemption is for organisations acting in the public interest and whose activities are directed towards a non-commercial purpose."

Tax evasion is illegal; tax avoidance is not, but the Tribunals and the Courts, it must be said at the behest of HMRC, are looking seriously at schemes that HMRC have decided can be described as "un-acceptable tax avoidance".

Cumbernauld Development Corporation v. The Commissioners of Customs & Excise (No. 14630) 6 November 2000

Although this appeal was made by Cumbernauld Development Corporation (CDC), the effect of the decision,

APPENDIX C

and indeed the negotiations preceding it, concerned Dullatur Golf Club (DGC).

The matter was reasonably simple – CDC needed land owned by DGC, which included their clubhouse, in order to complete the construction and road layout of the Cumbernauld New Town. In return for the land and buildings, CDC offered an alternative piece of land so that the existing course could be retained although on a totally different layout which resulted in two 18 hole courses. In addition a replacement clubhouse including leisure facilities and a manager/caretaker's flat was provided.

A formal agreement was reached based on the above arrangement and CDC agreed in it to pay for all planning and statutory fees. The total cost of the development was approximately £3m of which £1m related to the course and £2m to the clubhouse, associated car parking, and access. CDC obtained a valuation of £120,000 for the old clubhouse and its site. The question for the Tribunal was the valuation of the supply by the appellant, CDC, to DGC in circumstances where no money changed hands.

In a very lengthy decision, the Tribunal did not accept the contentions of either CDC or DGC that the true consideration was nil. The Tribunal followed the reasoning in *Empire Stores* that the subjective value was the value which the recipient attributes to what he received. The Tribunal found that the value of the consideration applicable to the transfer to CDC of the DGC clubhouse and land should be calculated subjectively by determining the value attributed by CDC to what they obtained – effectively the total cost of the development, £3m. The crude construction cost needed to be modified in respect of various undertakings given to DGC about membership, and maintenance of the additional golf course land they obtained. The matter was referred back to the parties to agree an appropriate value for VAT purposes taking on board the opinion of the Tribunal.

This is a particularly complex matter especially as both CDC and DGC are not entitled to recover all input VAT charged to them. The details need not be discussed here, but it is a warning to any golf club becoming involved with land exchanges, whether or not including buildings, that just because the value is agreed between the parties, HMRC do not have to accept that face value, and have powers to intervene if they consider that in addition to any cash exchanged, there are non-monetary considerations involved.

Northampton Theatre Trust [2006] BVC 2587

This appeal related to the introduction of The Cultural Services Order. It defines cultural services as a right of admission to a museum, gallery, art exhibition or zoo, or a theatrical, musical or choreographic performance of a cultural nature. VAT Notice 701/47 provided for refunds of VAT going back to 1st January 1990, subject to unjust enrichment, so that Customs, in the view of the Tribunal, had administratively applied the Cultural Services Order retrospectively.

The appellant had made two claims which had been rejected by Customs & Excise – one for the period 1st April 1993 to the 4th December 1996 (when the three-year cap was introduced) and one for the period 5th March 2001 to the 4th March 2004.

APPENDIX C

The Tribunal Chairman, John F. Avery Jones released his decision on the 3rd March 2006 and he considered that in the period covered by the first claim up to 31st May 1996 before the Cultural Services Order came into force, the Appellant had a Community right to repayment. He was of the view that the same necessarily applied to the periods after that date with both claims.

In his final paragraph he stated that

1. The Appellant would not be unjustly enriched if it kept the refund.

2. The Apellant is entitled to a refund for the period 1st April 1993 to the 4th December 1996 and the period 5th March 2001 to the 4th March 2004 as a Community right that is not affected by the three-year cap.

Default Surcharge Assessments

There are a number of VAT & Duties Tribunal appeals against default surcharge assessments (the late submission of VAT returns) which rest on their particular facts and they are not discussed here. In order to succeed, the club must show that it has a reasonable excuse for the late submission – reliance on a third party or a lack of funds is generally not accepted as a reasonable excuse.

Table of Cases

Abbotsley Golf and Squash Club Ltd v. Commissioners of Customs & Excise (No 15042) 79

Basingstoke and District Sports Trust Ltd v C & E Commrs. [1995] VATDR 405 61

Bridport & West Dorset Golf Club (TC 01214) 41, 66

Burntisland Golf House Club v. Commissioners of Customs & Excise (No 6340) 75

Canterbury Hockey Club and Canterbury Ladies Hockey Club v. The Commissioners for HM Revenue and Customs 71

Card Protection Plan v. Commissioners of Customs & Excise 30

Chipping Sodbury Golf Club (TC 02234) 42

Chobham Golf Club v. Commissioners of Customs & Excise (No 14867) 74

Copthorne Village Golf Club v. Commissioners of Customs & Excise (No 17426) 78

Cumbernauld Development Corporation v. The Commissioners of Customs & Excise (No. 14630) 81

De Vere Golf and Leisure Ltd and De Vere Group plc (No 18078) 73

Elsham Golf Club Ltd. v. Commissioners of Customs & Excise (No 18107) 77

Exeter Golf and Country Club [1981] STC 211 80

Fleming (trading as Bodycraft) v Revenue and Customs Commissioners; Condé Nast Publications Ltd v Revenue and Customs Commissioners ([2008] UKHL 2) 36

HP Bulmer Limited v J Bollinger SA [1974] Ch 401 43

Kennemer Golf & Country Club v. Staatssecretaris van Financien (Case C-174/00) 37, 70

Keswick Golf Club and others v. Commissioners of Customs & Excise (No 15493) 69

TABLE OF CASES

Marks & Spencer v Customs & Excise Commissioners (Case C-62/00) 35
Milnathort Golf Club v. Commissioners of Customs & Excise (No 17889) 76
Tall Pines Golf and Leisure Co. Ltd v. Commissioners of Customs & Excise (No 16538) 80
West Essex Golf Club v. Commissioners of Customs & Excise (No 7321) 79

Index

affiliation fees 19, 40
annual adjustment 45
anti-avoidance legislation. 17
artisans' golf club 19
Capital Goods Scheme 46
catering concession 26
charity
    events 30
    supplies made by 20
clubhouse
    construction 46
    dart board 24
    extension 46
    games rooms 24
    refurbishment 23, 29
    snooker table 24
commercial influence ....
    .... 17, 20, 74
competition 3, 5, 6, 69, 70
    entry fee 30
    open, entry fee 30
    prizes 31
        cash 32
        goods 31
        trophies 32
Customs & Excise. *See* HMRC

default surcharge assessments 84
de minimis limits 3, 9
direct attribution 23, 24
direct competition 40, 52
eligible body 13, 15, 30, 33, 78
    definition 17
    non-profit making 18
emoluments 21
English Golf Union 19
entry fees 3, 31, 77
evasion, deliberate 13
exempt supplies
    charities 20
    local authorities 20
    locker rooms 23
gaming machines 29
Golf club VAT cases
    Bridport & West Dorset Golf Club 42, 44, 66
    Canterbury Hockey Clubs 6, 10, 14, 18-20, 24, 27, 30, 35-39, 41, 49
    Chipping Sodbury Golf Club 42

INDEX

Chobham Golf Club 74
Cumbernauld Development Corporation 81
Copthorne Village Golf Club 78
De Vere Golf and Leisure Ltd 81
Dullatur Golf Club 82
Dyke Golf Club, The 42
Elsham Golf Club Ltd 24
Kennemer Golf & Country Club 37
Keswick Golf Club.35, 41, 70
Mendip Spring Golf & Country Club 42
Milnathort Golf Club 23
Northampton Theatre Trust. 41, 43
Tall Pines Golf and Leisure Co. Ltd 81
Trent Lock Golf Club 42

golf course
    letting of 32
    use of 19

golf professional14, 15, 32, 47
    prvate tuition 33

honoraria 21

income
    from bar 10
    from catering 10
    from visitors 10

input tax ....
  .3, 7, 9, 10, 23, 25-27, 29, 75
    attributable to taxable supplies 23
    exempt 10

inspection visit 2

local authority 1
    supplies made by 20

lotteries 29

members' club 1, 6, 19, 40
    bar 25
    catering 25
    steward 25

membership scheme 6

multiple-sports club 18

non-profit making organisations 5, 40

partial exemption ....
    .... 3, 9, 23, 45, 76, 77
    de minimis limits 3, 9
    special method 11
    standard method 11
    taxable percentage 46

private club 1

prizes 3, 31-32

recovery
    overpaid output tax35, 64
    underclaimed input tax35

special method 77

INDEX

SportsVAT liability
   sports Coaching 15
standard method 27, 76, 77
steward 26
subscriptions ... ix, 5, 7, 18, 19
taxable supplies .. 9, 23, 25, 77
   bar 23
   visitors' facilities 23
temporary members..............
   .... 5, 24, 27, 36, 69
tour operators 18
travel agents 18
trophies 3
Value Added Tax Act 1994 ...
   .... 9, 17

value of the supply of services 79
VAT
   inspection 2, 45
   liability 13
      fees 17
      joining fees 15
      social facilities 18
   overpaid 36, 41
   recovery 26
      steward's accommodation .. 26
   refund 7
   returns 13, 47
      late submission 84
visitors (*also see* temporary members) 1, 23, 25